D0699591

Presented To:

Denver-Aida
and Merritt

Presented By:

Gram Lois and Gramps too

Date:

Sept 1st 2019

God's Little Story Book of Amazing Adventures

HB HONOR BOOKS

Tulsa, Oklahoma

Stories based on the following Bible versions:

The Holy Bible, New International Version®. NIV®. Copyright © 1973, 1978, 1984 by International Bible Society. Used by permission of Zondervan Publishing House. All rights reserved.

The *King James Version* of the Bible.

God's Little Story Book of Amazing Adventures
ISBN 1-56292-004-9
Copyright © 2001 by Honor Books
P.O. Box 55388
Tulsa, OK 74155

Written by Sarah M. Hupp
Cover and Interior Design by Whisner Design Group
Illustrated by Lisa Browning

introduction

What fun it is to read about people in the Bible! They had such amazing adventures. That's why we've put many of them together in *God's Little Story Book of Amazing Adventures* just for you.

Put yourself in their shoes. Would you be as brave as one of Gideon's men who went into battle with just a horn, a lighted candle, and a pot? If a bear attacked your sheep, would you be as strong as David? What would it be like to escape with Joseph, Mary, and baby Jesus into Egypt? Would you help to look for Jesus if He were lost? Would you be amazed if the Holy Spirit appeared as flames of fire dancing on everyone's head?

With God's help, you can be just as brave and strong and smart as our Bible heroes. They were ordinary people just like you. God loves you just as much as He loved them. You can do great things for God too. So come on . . . let's read!

Contents

8

Noah's Big Boat

(Genesis 6:5-22)

Long ago people were mean to each other. They hated God. This made God sad. So God said He would destroy the world with a flood because the people were so mean and sinful. But God promised to keep Noah and his family safe.

Noah was a kind man who loved God. So God told Noah to build a big boat. He told him what kind of wood to use and what food to put in the boat. He told him to put animals in the boat too.

Noah did exactly what God said. And God kept
Noah, his family, and all the animals safe.

*Dear Lord, help me to be like Noah and
do what You want me to do. Amen.*

Laban's Tricks

(Genesis 30:25-43)

Jacob took care of Laban's sheep. One day Jacob said, "Please pay me what you owe me." So Jacob came up with an idea. He said, "The sheep will have babies soon. All sheep with dots and spots will be mine." He told Laban he could keep the rest.

13

When the sheep were born, there were lots and lots with dots and spots, but only a few sheep without spots! Laban tried to trick Jacob. He took many of the sheep. Then he said, "Wait for the sheep to have babies again. You can have the sheep with stripes. I will keep the rest."

Laban wasn't being fair. So God let the sheep have lots of striped babies! Laban's tricks didn't work. Jacob got what Laban owed him.

Dear Lord, help me always to be fair to others. Amen.

16

Fat and Skinny Cows

(Genesis 41)

One night the king of Egypt had a dream. He saw seven fat cows eating grass. Then seven skinny cows came along and ate the fat cows! The king asked Joseph to tell him what this dream meant.

17

Joseph said, "The fat cows are seven years when you'll have lots of food. The skinny cows are seven years when there won't be enough food. God says to save some food from the good years to use during the bad years."

The king was amazed. He put Joseph in charge of the country and did everything God said. And his people were saved.

Dear Lord, I'm glad You know the future and always do what You say You will do. Amen.

God Leads the Way

(Exodus 13:21-14:22)

God's people didn't use maps or flashlights to get to the Promised Land. During the day, God led them with a pile of clouds that reached from the ground to the sky. God also made a tall flame of fire to give them light at night.

21

God used the clouds and fire to lead His people. When the clouds or fire started moving, the people followed. When the clouds or fire stopped moving, the people stopped too.

God also used the clouds and fire to protect His people. He put the fire in front of the Egyptians so they wouldn't chase God's people into the sea.

Thank You, Lord, for leading
and protecting me too.
Amen.

Moses Holds His Hands Up

(Exodus 17:8-16)

On their way to the Promised Land, God's people met the people of Amalek. The Amalekites were mean to God's people. They tried to steal their animals and food. They tried to destroy their tents! This made God angry.

So God told His people to fight the
Amalekites. Moses stood on a hill and
watched the battle. Then something amazing
happened! When Moses held his rod up in
the air, God's people started to win
the battle.

But when Moses' hands went down, the Amalekites started to win. So two men helped Moses hold up his hands all day. God's people won the battle.

Thank You, Lord, for friends who help us do hard things.
Amen.

27

A Donkey Talks

(Numbers 22)

The king of Moab asked Balaam to visit him. He wanted Balaam to go and say bad things to hurt God's people. At first God told Balaam not to go. Later He decided to let Balaam go. But God told him to only do what He told him to do. Balaam got on his donkey to go.

29

But God didn't want Balaam to say bad things to hurt His people. So God sent an angel to stop Balaam. The angel stood in front of Balaam's donkey. Three times the donkey saw God's angel and stopped in the road. Three times Balaam hit his donkey to make it keep walking.

30

Then God let the donkey talk! The donkey asked, "Why are you hitting me?" Then Balaam saw the angel too. Balaam was sorry. He promised to only say good things about God's people.

Dear Lord, help me to do what pleases You every day. Amen.

31

The Sun Stands Still

(Joshua 10:1-28)

One day the armies of five kings started a fight with the people of Gibeon. The Gibeonites asked God's people for help. So God's people came to help them. God sent a hailstorm to help too.

33

The hail killed lots of enemy soldiers. But there were still lots of enemy soldiers left. So Joshua asked God for another favor. He asked God to make the sun shine until all of the bad soldiers were killed.

So God made the sun stand still in the sky. There was no afternoon or nighttime until God's people won the battle.

Dear Lord, You are more powerful than the sun. Thank You for taking good care of everything, including me! Amen.

35

Horns, Clay Pots, and Candles

(Judges 6–7)

The Midianites were mean to God's people. They stole their animals. They destroyed their food. Then God spoke to Gideon. God told Gideon how to fight the big Midianite army.

So Gideon did what God said. He got three hundred men. Each man had a horn and a lighted candle covered with a clay pot. When the Midianites were asleep, Gideon's men circled their tents.

Then Gideon and his men shouted! They blew
their horns. They broke the pots that covered
their candles. The noise and lights scared the
Midianites. They ran away. And they never
bothered God's people again.

*Dear Lord, please show me what to do when
I have problems too. Amen.*

39

David Fights a Bear

(1 Samuel 17:34-37)

When David was a little boy, he took care of his father's sheep. He had to find green grass for the sheep to eat. He had to find water for them too. David had to keep the sheep safe.

Wild animals tried to eat David's sheep. One day a bear came and took one of David's sheep. David chased the bear and hit it. The bear dropped the sheep and tried to bite David.

42

But David grabbed the bear's fur. He
fought the bear and killed it. God made
David brave and strong.

*Thank You, Lord, for helping me to be
brave and strong like David was. Amen.*

44

A True Friend

(1 Samuel 20)

Jonathan was the son of a king. David was the son of a shepherd. Jonathan and David were best friends. One day the king heard that God wanted David to be the next king rather than Jonathan. This made the king angry.

David told Jonathan that the king wanted to kill him. So Jonathan told David to hide behind some rocks. He said he would talk to his father. If the king wanted to kill David, Jonathan would shoot an arrow past the rocks. Then David would have to run far away and hide.

Sadly, the king was angry with David. David had to leave his home and his good friend. But Jonathan helped David escape.

Dear God, help me to be a good friend who helps others too. Amen.

The Birds Bring Supper

(1 Kings 16:29-17:6)

Elijah listened to God. He spoke God's words. Once Elijah went to wicked King Ahab. He said, "God will not send rain until you follow Him." Then God told Elijah to go and hide.

Elijah ran away. God helped Elijah hide
in some bushes. He hid beside a
stream. Elijah could drink water
from the stream when he was
thirsty. But what could
Elijah eat?

Something wonderful happened! God sent some birds to Elijah with food. The birds came every morning. The birds came every night too. So Elijah never went hungry.

Thank You, Lord, for giving me food to eat and water to drink. Amen.

Fire and Water

(1 Kings 18:16-39)

King Ahab and Queen Jezebel told God's people to worship a statue named Baal. So Elijah said, "Let's have a contest. Let's see whether God or Baal is the real God. Let's see who can send fire down on an offering."

Elijah and the prophets of Baal put offerings on Mount Carmel. Then the prophets of Baal began to pray, "O Baal! Send fire down on the mountain." They prayed all day.

But nothing happened. Then it was Elijah's turn.

Elijah put lots of water on his offering. Then he prayed, "Lord, let them know that You are the real God." God sent down fire on Elijah's offering. Even though it was wet, it burned! He is the true God!

Hooray, God! You are the only true God! You are stronger than anything! Amen.

Elijah and the Little Cloud

1 Kings 18:41-46

It hadn't rained for a long time. But Elijah told King Ahab that rain was coming. But when the king looked up into the sky, he didn't see any clouds. And neither did anyone else.

So Elijah prayed. Then he told his servant to look for clouds. But there were none. Six times Elijah sent his servant to look for clouds. Six times there were no clouds. Then his servant cried, "I see a little cloud!"

Elijah said, "Here comes the rain!"
And before everyone could get home,
the rain started, just like Elijah said
it would.

Thank You, Lord, for the rain that
keeps the rivers full and gives us
water to drink.
Amen.

59

Saved From Slavery

(2 Kings 4:1-7)

A woman owed a merchant a large amount of money. The merchant said, "Sell your sons as slaves. Then pay me what you owe me." But Elisha had a better idea. "What do you have in your house?" he asked.

61

"Only a jar of oil," the woman replied. So Elisha said, "God says to ask your friends for all their extra pots. Then come home and close your door. Get your oil jar, and pour oil into all the extra pots."

The woman did what God had said. She sold the extra oil and used the money to pay back the merchant. Her obedience saved her sons from slavery.

Help me, Lord, to do what You want me to do too. Amen.

Bumps and Lumps and Rashes

(2 Kings 5:1-14)

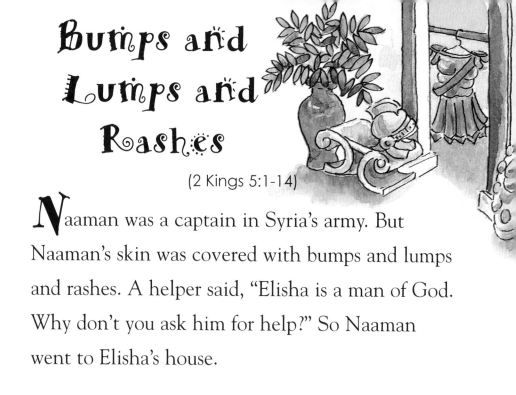

Naaman was a captain in Syria's army. But Naaman's skin was covered with bumps and lumps and rashes. A helper said, "Elisha is a man of God. Why don't you ask him for help?" So Naaman went to Elisha's house.

65

But Elisha wouldn't come outside. He sent another helper to tell Naaman to wash in the river seven times. This made Naaman angry. "If Elisha won't talk to me himself, I'm not going to do what he said," Naaman fussed. "Besides, I don't like the Jordan river."

Naaman's helper begged him to do what Elisha said. Finally, Naaman did. And when he came out of the river the last time, he was healed.

Thank You, Lord, for helping me feel better when I get sick too. Amen.

68

Jonah and the Big Fish

(Jonah 1–2)

God wanted Jonah to go to Nineveh to tell people to follow Him. But Jonah wouldn't go. He jumped on a boat and sailed the other way. So God sent a big storm. It almost sank the boat.

Jonah knew the storm was his fault. He told the captain, "Throw me into the water, and the storm will stop." The captain did what Jonah said, and the storm stopped! Then God sent a big fish to swallow Jonah.

Jonah spent three days in the fish's tummy.
He told God he was sorry for running away.
So God forgave Jonah. He made the fish spit
Jonah onto dry land.

*Dear Lord, help me do what
You want—always! Amen.*

Haman's Plan Backfires

(Esther 3 and 6)

Haman was a proud man. He wanted everyone to honor him. But Mordecai wouldn't bow to anyone but God. This made Haman angry. He wanted to kill Mordecai and his people. But Haman didn't know that the king liked Mordecai.

Once Mordecai stopped two men from killing the king. So the king gave Mordecai a robe and a special horse. The king chose Haman to walk in front of Mordecai. Haman had to tell everyone that the king was pleased with Mordecai.

Haman was mad. His plan didn't work. People didn't honor him anymore. They honored Mordecai. Mordecai had been helpful to the king and faithful to God too.

Dear Lord, I love You!
Help me to help others too. Amen.

An Escape at Night

(Matthew 2)

When Jesus was a baby, His family lived in Bethlehem. Wise men from the East came to visit Him. They brought gifts of gold and spices. After the wise men went home, God sent an angel to Joseph.

The angel said, "Herod wants to kill Jesus! Run now! Go to Egypt, and you will be safe." Though it was dark outside, Joseph did what the angel said. Mary, Joseph, and Jesus escaped before the sun came up.

That day soldiers came to Bethlehem. They wanted to kill baby Jesus. But Jesus and His family had escaped at night and were safe.

Thank You, God, for taking care of me just like You took care of Jesus. Amen.

Jesus is Lost

(Luke 2:41-52)

When Jesus was a boy, Mary and Joseph took Him to Jerusalem. They went to the temple for a feast. Soon it was time to go home. Mary and Joseph started walking. They thought Jesus was walking with some friends or other family members.

Later that day, Mary and Joseph looked for Jesus. He was not with His friends. He was not with His aunts or uncles. Jesus was lost! Mary and Joseph walked back to Jerusalem. They called, "Jesus! Where are You?"

Mary and Joseph looked and looked for Jesus.

Finally they went to the temple. There was Jesus!

He was talking to the teachers. Jesus was safe!

*Thank you, Lord, that I'm never lost with You.
You always know where I am. Amen.*

A Boatload of Fish

(Luke 5:1-11)

When Jesus was a grown-up, He walked to the seashore. He saw Peter, James, and John. They were fishermen. They were washing their fishnets. Jesus stepped into Peter's boat. He began to teach people about God.

Then Jesus told Peter to go out into the lake. He said, "Put your net in the water." Peter had been fishing all night long. He hadn't caught even one fish. But he did what Jesus said.

Immediately, fish jumped into Peter's net. Soon Peter's boat was full of fish. Jesus said, "Follow me! From now on you will catch men instead of fish!"

Lord, I want to follow You and tell others about You too. Amen.

The Wild Man in the Graveyard

(Mark 5:1-20)

A wild man lived in the graveyard. He was so strong! No chains or ropes could tie him up. Night and day the man cut himself with sharp stones. But one day the wild man saw Jesus. He ran up to Him.

Jesus was sad. He knew that evil spirits made the man wild. So Jesus told the evil spirits to go into some pigs. Then the pigs went wild! They ran down a steep hill and drowned in the sea.

Now the man wasn't wild anymore. He smiled at Jesus. Jesus said, "Tell your friends what God has done for you." And the man did.

Dear Lord, help me tell my friends what
You have done for me too.
Amen.

Fishing for Taxes

(Matthew 17:24-27)

A tax collector from the temple came to Peter. He wanted Peter to pay the temple tax. The tax collector wanted Jesus to pay taxes too. So Peter told Jesus about the tax collector.

So Peter went fishing. The fish he caught had money in its mouth just like Jesus had said! So Peter paid his taxes and Jesus' taxes too.

Dear Lord, help me to trust that You will always provide everything I need too. Amen.

i Want it Now!

(Luke 15:11-32)

Jesus told a story about a man who had two sons. The younger son was selfish. He said, "Father, you said you would give me some money when you die. But I want it now!"

97

The father gave the young son his money, and the son left home.

He had parties every day. But soon all of his money was gone. The younger son had no place to live. He was cold, hungry, and alone.

The younger son decided to go home. He asked his father to forgive him. And the father gladly did because he loved his son very much.

Dear Lord, my family loves me too. Help me not to be selfish. Amen.

The Holy Spirit Comes

(Acts 1–2)

Jesus had gone back to Heaven. So His followers met together to pray. Suddenly they heard a mighty wind. Whoosh! Little flames of fire danced on everyone's heads too. God had sent the Holy Spirit to them!

101

Then they all started talking in different languages that they had never learned. They all wanted to tell others about Jesus. They were so happy! People outside thought they were having a party.

Then Jesus' followers went outside. They told everyone about Jesus. Three thousand people believed in Jesus that day!

Hooray for You, God! Hooray for the Holy Spirit! I want to tell others about Jesus too. Amen.

103

Blinded by the Roadside

(Acts 9:1-19)

Christians are people who believe in Jesus. Saul didn't like Christians. He thought that Christians didn't do what God's law said. So Saul was mean to them. He put anyone who believed in Jesus into jail.

One day Saul was walking along a road. Suddenly a light from Heaven blasted through the clouds. The light was so bright! It hurt Saul's eyes. Then Saul heard the Lord's voice ask, "Why are you being so mean?"

For three days Saul couldn't see. But God sent a man to tell Saul about Jesus. Then Saul believed in Jesus too. And God let Saul see again.

Thank you, Lord, that I can see with my eyes too. Amen.

107

A Runaway Comes Home

(Philemon)

While Paul was in prison, he met Onesimus. Onesimus was a servant who had run away from his master. Paul told Onesimus about Jesus, and Onesimus became a believer. But then Paul said Onesimus should go back to his master.

Onesimus was afraid. The law said that a runaway servant could be killed. So Paul wrote a letter to Onesimus's master. He asked the master to be kind. He asked him to forgive Onesimus just like God forgives us.

Onesimus took the letter and went home.

And his master was kind and forgave him.

Thank You, God, for forgiving me just like

Onesimus's master forgave him.

Help me to forgive others when they do bad
things to me too. Amen.

If you have enjoyed this book, or if it has
impacted your life, we would like to hear from you.
Please contact us at:

Honor Books
Department E
P.O. Box 55388
Tulsa, Oklahoma 74155
Or by e-mail at info@honorbooks.com

Additional copies of this book and other titles
in the *God's Little Story Book* series
are available from your local bookstore.